Written & Illustrated by
Bronwyn Olson

All Scripture references
taken from the King
James Version of the
Bible.

Sonshine for the Broken (c) Bronwyn Olson 2024

ISBN: 978-1-923122-99-4 (Paperback)

All rights reserved. No part of this publication may be reproduced, stored in a retrieval system, or transmitted in any form or by any means electronic, mechanical, photocopying, recording, or otherwise, without the prior written permission of the author.

Published in Australia by Bronwyn Olson
and InHouse Publishing.
www.inhousepublishing.com.au

Dedication

Life is not a solitary journey and as much as we may try, we don't function completely apart from other human interaction and it's those wonderful interactions that help formulate our own journey, the direction we go, the choices we make and the trials we are able to endure with the courage and joy those special ones bring to our lives. With that in mind, I dedicate this book to my amazing husband, Pat, who like a gentle stream quietly refreshes my soul and comforts me in my grief, reminding me of who I am in Christ and helping to rewrite the narrative in my head. I also dedicate it to my dear prayer group friends who faithfully pray with and for me, laugh with me and weep with me and are truly like sisters to me. Finally and most importantly, I dedicate it to my dear Saviour, Jesus, my best friend and Lord. The lover of my soul!

My hope for this book is that the reader will walk straight past me

—

into the arms of Jesus.

Preface

The Bible says in Psalm 119:130a, "The entrance of thy words giveth light." That is why you'll find amongst my own thoughts and experiences plenty of verses from God's Word and what He thinks about things. For when we are suffering and in the dark, what do we need more than the Light. Light reveals what's in the dark and can show us the road back to wholeness through the truth. Jesus said, "I am the light of the world; he that followeth me shall not walk in darkness, but shall have the light of life" (John 8:12). He also said in John 14:6, "I am the way, the truth and the life: no man cometh unto the Father, but by Me."

This book can be used in a number of ways, either a read-through book where you might just sit and read cover to cover, or you might read a section a day - like a devotional or as a coffee-table book where you pick it up as the desire arises and hopefully find a little gem to brighten your day. However you choose to read it, I pray it blesses you and does bring light to your heart from the Light-Giver Himself - Jesus.

Table of Contents

Near to the Brokenhearted 11
The Creator of All Things 14
Waiting on the Lord – Part 1 16
Waiting on the Lord – Part 2 18
Be Like the Cockatoo! 24
Walk in the Light 29
Standing in the Rain 30
Let Go and Let God 32
Truth on Suffering – Part 1 34
Truth on Suffering – Part 2 36
Truth on Suffering – Part 3 38
Truth on Suffering – Part 4 40
Truth on Suffering – Part 5 41
Truth on Suffering – Part 6 44
Truth on Suffering – Part 7 46
A Living Testimony 47
Broken Pottery 48
Let the Light Shine Through 52
Who I Am 54
His Beautiful Creation or Discarded Things? 56
The Apple of His Eye 60
Abundant Life You Can Find 62
Who's Your Influencer – Part 1 66
Who's Your Influencer – Part 2 69
Who's Your Influencer – Part 3 72
Beyond God's Love 75
The Little Pottery Vase 76
How to be Saved – Roman's Road 78
References 80
About the Author 81

Near to the Brokenhearted

Lord, thank you for the pain that cuts deep in my heart – not because I like pain and to feel such hurt, but because you have taught me the joy of Your presence and I know how this pain drives me back into your arms every time. You're the only one who truly understands and can do anything about it! Loved ones can do their best to support me and be there, but you alone know the depths of my heart and the sorrow of my soul.

What breaks your heart? For me it's the pain of a child that was incredibly difficult to raise as a single mum until she was 8 and not knowing 'til she was 12 that her behaviour was due to her having a substantial portion of the alphabet in conditions, including autism, I had previously thought were just nice ways of saying you had a defiant and difficult child. Then to have her walk away from her step-dad and I at the age of 17 because we wouldn't call her a different pronoun and validate a lifestyle contrary to what is clearly set out in the Bible, has been incredibly painful and a steep curve in learning to live in the desert, hanging on to the only source of hope and anchor to the soul – Jesus.

Near to the Brokenhearted   (Continued)

Now, almost 2 years later, the pain doesn't go away, but I have learnt to sing in the storm, rejoice in the pain and to realise what a powerful offering to the Lord my pain-filled cries to Him truly are. See Psalm 50:23.

Thankfully, I've never really been one to blame God for my pain for I have always blamed others or myself, but for those of you who do struggle with this, remember we live in a world where God has given everyone 'free will' to choose their own path and unfortunately that commonly means a path without Him. However, He loved us so much He sent His One and Only Son, Jesus to be the payment for our sins and to give us eternal life. So whatever lies tell you that He doesn't care, He's to blame for your pain remember this and call out to Him. His Word says, He is near to the broken-hearted (Psalm 34:18).

It doesn't mean everyday is easy and the pain doesn't hurt, but what it can mean - if you let Him come into your heart and hold you, is that you will know a love that leaves you speechless! You will truly see how tenderly He wants to hold you in your pain and make beauty from your ashes. Will you pray with me now?

Near to the Brokenhearted (Continued)

Jesus, I'm in so much pain I don't know what to do or why I have to suffer this injustice. It hurts so much. I know you are Sovereign Lord of everything and yet so near to the brokenhearted. In fact, you're right here in this room, yearning to comfort me and hold me close. Hold me Jesus, heal my broken heart. By your Spirit, I invite you into this situation to do something beautiful with my ashes, to help me be a light in the dark so that others too would know Your great love and be healed. For we know one day we will be in Heaven with you and every tear will be wiped away, so until that day keep me safe in your arms. I love you Jesus!

> "He healeth the broken
> in heart and bindeth
> up their wounds."
> Psalm 147:3

The Creator of all Things

Matthew 14:15-18

And when it was evening, His disciples came to Him saying, This is a desert place, and the time is now past; send the multitude away, that they may go into the villages, and buy themselves victuals. But Jesus said unto them, They need not depart; give ye them to eat. And they say unto Him, We have here but five loaves, and two fishes. He said, Bring them hither to Me.

The Creator of all Things

Do you stand in the wilderness,
begging God for bread?
Wondering at His promise
to do all that He has said.
The disciples thought the same way,
many years ago
– puzzled at their problem,
but little did they know.
Standing there before them,
the Creator of all things.
He was able to sustain them
and with Him abundance bring.
Feeding the thousands
that crowded, on that day
or answering a desperate prayer,
'Lord, how will we find a way?'
Remember He is with you
and lacks no strength or power!
He sees your every need and
has already provided for this hour.
So trust when the horizon
appears desolate and alone.
He's already sent out power
from His heavenly throne.
And as you kneel before Him,
the answer it will come
and you'll rise up hallelujah!
To His embrace you'll run!

Waiting on the Lord - Part 1

Exodus 32:1
And when the people saw that Moses delayed to come down out of the mount, the people gathered themselves together unto Aaron, and said unto him, Up, make us gods, which shall go before us; for as for this Moses, the man that brought us up out of the land of Egypt, we wot not what is become of him.

Lamentations 3:25-26
The LORD is good unto them that wait for Him, To the soul that seeketh him. It is good that a man should both hope and quietly wait for the salvation of the Lord.

Waiting on the Lord - Part 1

Many times it is easier to fall back on what we know, to trust the familiar and not to wait on God. Waiting can seem so hard and fill us with worry. When the road ahead seems unclear, difficult or uncertain, it can be easy to take things into our own hands, and run back to unhealthy relationships, and habits; even when we know they are contrary to the Bible and thus God's will. We can start to doubt He is at work in our lives and that His plans for us are good and come up with a 'plan B' just as the children of Israel did in the wilderness when they felt Moses had been up the mountain too long. See Exodus 32.

Unfortunately, I made this mistake when I was younger, frustrated with waiting, I compromised and settled for the immediacy of an 'ok' relationship that quickly turned to an abusive relationship. It brought me lots of pain and consequences that I still live with.

What about you? Do you think the Lord is taking too long, to do something in your life or to answer your prayers? Or do you feel that He has somehow forgotten you? It may feel like a good idea to satisfy your longing with the immediate, but settling for anything other than God's best will only bring heartache and trouble. It is good to wait on the Lord!

Waiting on the Lord - Part 2

Exodus 32:2-5
And Aaron said unto them, Break off the golden earrings, which are in the ears of your wives, of your sons, and of your daughters, and bring them unto me. And all the people brake off the golden earrings which were in their ears, and brought them unto Aaron. And he received them at their hand, and fashioned it with a graving tool, after he had made it a molten calf: and they said, These be thy gods, O Israel, which brought thee up out of the land of Egypt. And when Aaron saw it, he built an altar before it; and Aaron made proclamation, and said, Tomorrow is a feast to the Lord.

Exodus 32:19-20
And it came to pass, as soon as he (Moses) came nigh unto the camp, that he saw the calf, and the dancing: and Moses' anger waxed hot, and he cast the tables (10 commandments) out of his hands, and brake them beneath the mount. And he took the calf which they had made, and burnt it in the fire, and ground it to powder, and strawed it upon the water, and made the children of Israel drink it.

Exodus 32:35
And the Lord plagued the people, because they made the calf, which Aaron made.

Waiting on the Lord – Part 2

Now, we'd like to think after all Aaron had seen the Lord do, he would have violently protested and admonished them to worship only the Lord, but sadly you'll see (Exodus 32) he went right along with it and had to answer to both Moses and the Lord as to why he would do such a thing! If you didn't read on you might think, well Aaron's done his dash. God's not going to use him anymore and we could be justified to give him some very unflattering labels – betrayer, loser, disappointment, but thanks be to God, the story doesn't end here!

Now in Chapter 40 of Exodus, we see the Tabernacle (God's holy meeting place) is completed and erected. Moses then is to take the "anointing oil, and anoint the tabernacle, all that is therein, and shalt hallow it, and all the vessels thereof: and it shall be holy" (Exodus 40:9b). This is God's holy house on earth, so surely you would want a very 'holy' person for the role of high priest, the one to intercede for the people before God and manage the running of His sanctuary thus ensuring he, the other priests and workers in the tabernacle and all the people, offered their sacrifices correctly and met God's requirements for sin under the law. So are you as surprised as me that God chose Aaron?

Waiting on the Lord – Part 2   (Continued)

Exodus 39:27a,30
And they made coats of fine linen of woven work for Aaron, and for his sons...And they made the plate of the holy crown of pure gold, and wrote upon it a writing, like to the engravings of a signet, Holiness To The Lord.

Exodus 40:13-15
And thou shalt put upon Aaron the holy garments, and anoint him, and sanctify him; that he may minister unto me in the priest's office. And thou shalt bring his sons, and clothe them with coats: and thou shalt anoint them, as thou didst anoint their father, that they may minister unto Me in the priest's office: for their annointing shall surely be an everlasting priesthood throughout their generations.

Exodus 40:34
Then a cloud covered the tent of the congregation, and the glory of the LORD filled the tabernacle.

Waiting on the Lord – Part 2 (Continued)

God tells Moses, in Exodus 40:12-13 to take Aaron and his sons and wash them and set them apart for the Lord's work. Here, Aaron who had betrayed God, is now clothed in fine linen (signifying purity and strength) and crowned with a gold crown labelled, 'Holiness to the LORD.' Appointed as God's high priest, and his sons priests and continuing down his family line, it's important to see Aaron couldn't make himself clean – God set him apart.

This is a foreshadowing of the grace that would come through our Lord Jesus, who would become the sacrifice, once and for all (instead of needing the daily sacrifices of countless animals) to pay the price for ALL sin so that we too could become holy to the Lord! "For He hath made Him to be sin for us, who knew no sin; that we might be made the righteousness of God in Him" (2 Corinthians 5:21).

What about you? Are you carrying some ugly labels? Labels that keep you looking down, not worthy to look up into the eyes of the Eternal? If that is your story there is truth, grace and forgiveness at the foot of the cross. Wonderful, matchless grace that can wash away your past and make you completely new, showing you who you're really supposed to be and what God really thinks of you! God's grace upon Aaron is amazing and should encourage us to "come boldly to the throne of grace to find help in time of need" (Hebrews 4:16a).

Waiting on the Lord – Part 2 (Continued)

If, like me, you have accepted Jesus as Lord and Saviour, you can stand on the truth of 1 Peter 2:9. He has taken us out of our dirty, sinful state and made us royal, chosen and set apart! This doesn't mean we are sinless and won't let God down at times, or sometimes feel contrary to this, but because of Jesus' perfection and sacrifice, it's not based on our performance, but rather Christ's victory on the cross! We are covered by His blood and made clean and can stand on His promises!

Dear Lord, thank you for your wonderful, redeeming love! Thank you that Christ died for us while we were still sinners and that because of your wonderful grace we can enjoy all the benefits of belonging to you. Thank you that you call us chosen, redeemed, loved, holy to the Lord, a royal priesthood. Please reveal any names written on my head that are not from you and in your wonderful name, wash those labels away so that only Your truth about me remains. I pray this in the mighty name, the only name that can forgive sins and heal all our diseases, Jesus!

Waiting on the Lord – Part 2 (Continued)

Hebrews 4:14-16
Seeing then that we have a great high priest, that is passed into the heavens, Jesus the Son of God, let us hold fast our profession. For we have not an high priest which cannot be touched with the feeling of our infirmities; but was in all points tempted like as we are, yet without sin. Let us therefore come boldly unto the throne of grace, that we may obtain mercy, and find grace to help in time of need.

1 Peter 2:9
But ye are a chosen generation, a royal priesthood, an holy nation, a peculiar people; that ye should shew forth the praises of Him who hath called you out of darkness into His marvellous light.

Romans 5:8
But God commendeth His love toward, in that, while we were yet sinners, Christ died for us.

1 John 1:7
But if we walk in the light as He is in the light, we have fellowship one with another, and the blood of Jesus Christ, His Son cleanseth us from all sin.

Be Like the Cockatoo!

Proverbs 3:5-6
Trust in the Lord with all your heart; and lean not on thine own understanding. In all thy ways acknowledge Him and He shall direct thy paths.

Psalm 37:23-24
The steps of a good man are ordered by the LORD: And he delighteth in his way. Though he fall, he shall not be utterly cast down: For the LORD upholdeth him with his hand.

Be Like the Cockatoo!

I think I can target the exact moment it starts to fall apart for me – when I go from walking in the Sonshine of my Saviour, enjoying His encouraging and loving gaze upon my face to looking around at others' journeys and worrying that I'm falling behind, that I'm no good compared to them and that I will never 'make it' in the thing I believe God wants me to pursue, the things I do for Him.

If I could only train myself to keep looking up, to keep trusting His voice, His direction, His Spirit then I would save myself so much heartache and worry! In fact, those sweet moments when I'm in communion with Him, and expressing my heartfelt gratitude for His goodness and awe at His power and Sovereignty in my life, I know amazing joy and happiness – for the clay is not fighting the potter but letting Him create the little cup I'm meant to be – both unique and priceless!

Can you relate? Do you find those moments when you feel free to be who God created you to be? A unique child of God, submitted to His will for your life and trusting Him fully?

I still remember years ago seeing a video on youtube that highlights this so well! A performer in Las Vegas – of all places, had a collection of Australian birds including a sulphur-crested cockatoo, a magpie, and a pink and grey galah. He had trained these birds to do lots of different tricks and increasingly harder little tasks.

Be Like the Cockatoo!   (Continued)

It was obvious he loved the birds and had a strong bond with them, but what really struck me was the implicit trust the sulphur-crested cockatoo had in his trainer. For the performer decided to do some juggling and not just with juggling balls, but with the cockatoo as well! First, He asked the bird who was sitting on his hand to play dead, which the bird did remarkably well - not a twitch or flutter - he looked cactus! Next the performer proceeded to throw the bird high in the air, along with the juggling balls —tossing him up in coordination with the three balls, in a very spectacular fashion! Every time the performer threw the cockatoo into the air, he caught him again. The bird never flinched, looked around, or worried about whether his trainer would catch him again. He placed all his trust in him and knew he only had to do his part —and his trainer caught him without fail!

What a beautiful picture of the trust we can have in Jesus! It challenged me that a little sulphur-crested cockatoo had more faith than most followers of Jesus. He knew where and in whom to place his trust, what his role in the show was and that his trainer was going to catch him without fail! The cockatoo didn't look around at all the distractions - cameras, faces in the crowd - THE OTHER BIRDS, but he stayed completely in sync with his trainer and listened and obeyed his voice.

Be Like the Cockatoo! (Continued)

Lord, help us be like this sulphur-crested cockatoo. Help us to understand our role in the Christian life, that we are small and frail like a cockatoo, but You are strong, trustworthy and good and You will catch us every time! Help us to make it a habit to look to You, to hear Your voice and drown out the noise of the world with all it's distractions! Lord, that we may spend quiet time with You in the easy moments so when the hard ones come we have learnt to listen only to You and know You will never let us down.

Be Like the Cockatoo! (Continued)

My sheep hear my voice, and I know them, and they follow me: And I give unto them eternal life; and they shall never perish, neither shall any man pluck them out of my hand.
John 10:27-28

Walk in the Light

I want to walk the path
that shines brighter everyday.
I want to feel your nearness,
every time I pray.
I want to leave this world behind,
run with You,
whose Faithful and Kind.
Feel your wind blow through
this mortal flesh.
Filled by your Spirit,
knowing Your way is best.
And day by day, as I take each step
Less of this world's track beneath me I feel.
I look down at my feet —
see a shining, crystal path,
That leads me to Glory,
my forever home at last!

Standing in the Rain

John 10:10
The thief cometh not, but for to steal, and to kill, and to destroy: I am come that they might have life, and that they might have it more abundantly.

Standing in the Rain

Standing in the rain
You may feel nothing but pain.
Wondering how life, from this empty shell
can bloom. Your garden a desolate tomb.
But I am here to testify, God can
 – when to self you die.
Let Him take your empty tomb,
once again make that garden bloom.
But this time it will grow stronger,
bloom brighter, last longer.
For when you give your life to Him,
He works without and works within.
He roots out anything that harms,
Instils hope, your fears He calms.
Leaving only what is good and true.
to make His life bloom through you.

Let Go and Let God

Let Go and Let God

When you let go and let God,
when you press in in faith
Whe you pray first,
before anything else
When you yearn for God like nobody else
When you hunger for the Bible
– just one minute more!
When you thirst for revival
—-a glimpse of heaven's open door
When you throw your whole self
in faith at His feet
When you look for His presence
in all that you meet.
When you strain for His voice,
so familiar and kind
When you're quick to love others
and try to be kind
Then you will enter a realm of your own
Where Heaven's so real
 -you see Him on His throne
Where miracles happen,
each moment, each hour
Where you experience God's
greatness and power
Where doors open
that before you'd not even seen
And where your heart beats with His
What a heavenly dream!

Truth on Suffering – Part 1

Isaiah 53:5
But he was wounded for our transgressions, he was bruised for our iniquities: the chastisement of our peace was upon him; and with his stripes we are healed.

John 19:14-17
And it was the preparation of the passover, and about the sixth hour: and he saith unto the Jews, Behold your King! But they cried out, Away with him, away with him, crucify him. Pilate saith unto them, Shall I crucify your King? The chief priests answered, We have no king but Caesar. Then delivered he him therefore unto them to be crucified. And they took Jesus, and led him away. And he bearing his cross went forth into a place called the place of a skull, which is called in the Hebrew Golgotha:

John 14:26
But the Comforter, which is the Holy Ghost, whom the Father will send in my name, he shall teach you all things, and bring all things to your remembrance, whatsoever I have said unto you.

Truth on Suffering – Part 1

I find my heartache, my past, the things that aren't right in my life – family who doesn't talk to me, children who don't want to be in my life; all these things have this tendency to draw me into a vortex of grief and self-focus as I try to process the pain. However, today reading this heartbreaking passage about my Saviour's WILLING sacrifice for me (John 19), I'm powerfully reminded of these 7 things about suffering:

1: Suffering is not unique to us as humans for Jesus also suffered. The Lord Jesus left His throne in Heaven, His perfect kingdom where He was rightly loved, honoured and respected to be despised, rejected and ultimately killed for this broken world. He did this in order to bring redemption and healing through His payment of the price for sin and to give the gift of the Comforter who would come and live inside each individual believer. "Seeing then that we have a great high priest, that is passed into the heavens, Jesus the Son of God, let us hold fast our profession. For we have not an high priest which cannot be touched with the feeling of our infirmities; but was in all points tempted like as we are, yet without sin. Let us therefore come boldly unto the throne of grace, that we may obtain mercy and find grace to help in time of need" (Hebrews 4:14-16).

Truth on Suffering – Part 2

Genesis 2:16-17
And the Lord God commanded the man, saying, Of every tree of the garden thou mayest freely eat: But of the tree of the knowledge of good and evil, thou shalt not eat of it: for in the day that thou eatest thereof thou shalt surely die.

Genesis 3:1
Now the serpent was more subtil than any beast of the field which the Lord God had made. And he said unto the woman, Yea, hath God said, Ye shall not eat of every tree of the garden?

Genesis 3:6
And when the woman saw that the tree was good for food, and that it was pleasant to the eyes, and a tree to be desired to make one wise, she took of the fruit thereof, and did eat, and gave also unto her husband with her; and he did eat.

John 3:16
For God so loved the world, that He gave His only begotten Son, that whosoever believeth in Him should not perish, but have everlasting life.

Truth on Suffering – Part 2

2: When God did His most beautiful work of creating this world, you and I and all the beauty it contains, He never planned for us to suffer.

People often confuse God's sovereignty (His all powerfulness) with His justice. For how can He be a just God if He is all powerful, but lets people suffer? If He can stop a psychopath shooting a gun, stop the drunk from getting in that car and killing a pedestrian, why doesn't He? Here is where we need to ask what about free will. Where would be our choice to choose Him out of love? Wouldn't we all be just very elaborate robots or Emmets in a suped-up Lego world (The Lego Movie 2014:Warner Home Video), where God sat above us and jumped in whenever we weren't following the rules, so nobody got hurt?

If we go back to the garden of Eden, we see God had created a perfect world, in fact on the sixth day "God saw all that he had made, and it was very good" (Genesis 1:31a). Then in a moment of doubting God's Word, perfection was lost and sin entered paradise. We have been under the weight of sin's burden ever since, but praise be to God, He had a plan all along and sent Jesus to pay the price for our sin and buy us back and for those of us who receive His gift give us eternal life in Heaven with Him!

The Truth on Suffering – Part 3

Judges 10:6
And the children of Israel did evil again in the sight of the Lord, and served Baalim, and Ashtaroth, and the gods of Syria, and the gods of Zidon, and the gods of Moab, and the gods of the children of Ammon, and the gods of the Philistines, and forsook the Lord, and served not him.

2 Chronicles 7:14
If my people, which are called by my name, shall humble themselves, and pray, and seek my face, and turn from their wicked ways; then will I hear from heaven, and will forgive their sin, and will heal their land.

Isaiah 30:18
And therefore will the Lord wait, that he may be gracious unto you, and therefore will he be exalted, that he may have mercy upon you: for the Lord is a God of judgment: blessed are all they that wait for him.

Isaiah 61:3
To appoint unto them that mourn in Zion, to give unto them beauty for ashes, the oil of joy for mourning, the garment of praise for the spirit of heaviness; that they might be called trees of righteousness, the planting of the Lord, that he might be glorified.

The Truth on Suffering - Part 3

3: Suffering can and often does lead us closer to God and sweet communion with Him. For it's through our suffering that we come to the end of ourselves and realise our need for God. Time and time again, this is evident in Old Testament Israel as she becomes prosperous, then forgets God and turns to idols and relies on her own abilities and self-effort. Then God has to send trials: often a conquering army to bring about suffering and repentance. Does that sound familiar to us today? How often do people only cry out to God when they are suffering, desperate, and at the end of themselves? Sometimes it takes a harrowing experience to open our eyes to our need for God and how much He wants to be in our lives and reveal His truth to us - see Part 4.

If we can let God use our suffering to show His great love and mercy in our time of need we will be changed beyond what we can imagine as we start to grasp the depths of His amazing love and the efforts He will go to to bring us safely home. Will you invite Him into your pain and grief today? Let Him make beauty out of your ashes and bring healing with which none can compare.

The Truth on Suffering – Part 4

4: God will allow suffering in order to bring us to salvation. For what is the point of it all if we have a great life for the short time we're here on earth — Job said, "My days are swifter than a post (a runner), they flee away, they see no good" (Job 9:25) and then we die without knowledge of God and of His love and redeeming grace? Jesus said in John 10:10 "I am come that they might have life and that they might have it more abundantly."

So often we live for the temporal, the now, the stuff we can have, the relationships that make us feel good, our family, our success, but all these things are fleeting and can change in an instant. It's only our spirit that will go on forever into eternity whether that be with Christ or without Him. He therefore uses suffering in this life to disrupt our dependence on all the things I mentioned above and make us question what matters in life and what life actually is.

The Truth on Suffering – Part 5

5: For this is the greatest mystery of 'life' that it truly can only be found and fully experienced when in commune with its Maker. Just as a forgotten language cannot have meaning til it's code has been deciphered, a human creation can never understand their worth, their purpose, their origin until they have met the One who put each cell into motion and breathed His life-giving breath into their lungs. As they walk with Him and allow His Spirit to reveal the deep secrets of His love, that only an intimate relationship can foster, then they truly understand 'what is life'. "For you died, and your life is now hidden with Christ in God" (Colossians 3:3).

What I died? I thought you said this was about living! Yes, hang in there to the end and you will begin to see! For we see this truth played out in the natural world as well as here in the spiritual. An apt example, that perfectly illustrates this would be that of marriage — a new life of union between a man and a woman. In order for this to happen a man and woman must turn their back on their old life of being single man and single woman to becoming one in the union of marriage. See Genesis 2:24

I'm sure lots of us have probably known a couple where the marriage didn't go too well due to one or both parties still living the old way and treating their marriage as an 'add on' to their current status. They tie the knot, but still live seperate lives and only come together when it's

The Truth on Suffering – Part 5 (Continued)

Genesis 2:24
Therefore shall a man leave his father and mother and shall cleave unto his wife; and they shall become one flesh.

Romans 6:4-6
Therefore we are buried with Him by baptism into death: that like as Christ was raised up from the dead by the glory of the Father, even so we also should walk in the likeness of His resurrection. For if we have been planted together in the likeness of His death, we shall be also in the likeness of His resurrection. Knowing that our old man is crucified with him, that the body of sin might be destroyed, that henceforth we should not serve sin.

Romans 6:22-23
But now being made free from sin, and become servants to God, ye have your fruit unto holiness, and the end everlasting life. For the wages of sin is death; but the gift of God is eternal life through Jesus Christ our Lord.

Matthew 11:28-29
Come unto Me all ye that labour and are heavy laden and I will give you rest. Take my yoke upon you and learn of Me for I am meek and lowly in heart: and ye shall find rest unto your souls.

The Truth on Suffering – Part 5 (Continued)

convenient. This is a sad attempt at the beauty God had in mind when He created Eve for Adam and conversely Adam for Eve. They were to be an example of Christ and the church (made up of individual believers like us). Christ loved the church and gave Himself for it as we have read above and so should be a husband and wife's devotion and love for one another.

All this to explain Colossians 3:3 above. In order to receive God's wonderful life you must first be prepared to lay down your old life, old desires, old patterns and old relationships that no longer fit the bill in order to make room for all that God has for you in Christ. For I can tell you after being a Christian for over 30 years, you can never 'outdo' God! So lay down your meagre life that seems so important and very quickly you will get a God perspective of how really small life is without Him at the centre and that nothing, absolutely nothing can fill the longing, the hopes, the dreams in your heart like Christ. He will always amaze you and leave you in awe at His love, His wonder and His beauty if you are just willing.

The Truth on Suffering - Part 6

Psalm 56:3-4, 8-11
What time I am afraid, I will trust in thee. In God I will praise his word, in God I have put my trust; I will not fear what flesh can do unto me. Every day they wrest my words: All their thoughts are against me for evil.... (8) Thou tellest my wanderings: Put thou my tears into thy bottle: Are they not in Thy book? When I cry unto thee, then shall mine enemies turn back: This I know; for God is for me. In God will I praise His word: In the LORD will I praise His word. In God have I put my trust: I will not be afraid what man can do unto me.

Revelation 21:4-5
And God shall wipe away all tears from their eyes; and then shall be no more death, neither sorrow, nor crying, neither shall there be anymore pain; for the former things are passed away. Then He that sat upon the throne said, "Behold, I will make all things new. And he said unto me, Write: for these words are true and faithful."

Matthew 19:29
And everyone that hath forsaken houses, or brethren, or sisters, or father, or mother, or wife, or children, or lands for my name's sake, shall receive an hundredfold, and shall inherit everlasting life.

The Truth on Suffering – Part 6

6: Our suffering is not in vain and doesn't go unnoticed by God. In fact, every tear is caught in His bottle and He lovingly promises that in heaven all our tears will be wiped away and shall be no more and He will make all things new. And when we suffer for Him and for His name, He promises wonderful treasure in Heaven and encourages us that He has gone to prepare a place for us – in fact a mansion! I don't know about you, but on the days I feel low and unsure of where we'll live (we currently live in our caravan and have no fixed address, and no other worldly possessions), to know my Saviour has gone to prepare me my very own place with Him in Heaven beats anything I can compare it to for my short time here on earth!

We must always bring ourselves back to this point — that our Saviour and God has made a way for us to be restored and made whole as we are indwelt by His Spirit and set free from the power of sin and darkness. That at the end of this very short life we live here on earth - "a vapour that appeareth for a little time, then vanisheth away" (James 4:14b), we shall be reunited with Him and any saved family and friends for eternity in Heaven to experience joy and gladness evermore!

The Truth on Suffering - Part 7

7: Finally, the suffering that you have endured can help another to navigate their own road of suffering and to find the indescribable hope that you have in Christ for themselves. So be bold and share your story with someone today! I'm always amazed when I start to tell people 'about my crazy life' thinking they might label me as a bit weird and yet they turn around and thank me for sharing what God is doing in my life and how far He has bought me because it encourages them. So go and be a living testimony for Jesus!

> Blessed be God, even the Father of our Lord Jesus Christ, the Father of mercies, and the God of all comfort; Who comforteth us in all our tribulation, that we may be able to comfort them which are in any trouble, by the comfort wherewith we ourselves are comforted of God. For as the sufferings of Christ abound in us, so our consolation also aboundeth by Christ.
> 2 Corinthians 1:3-5

A Living Testimony...

You may be the only Bible someone ever meets;
and you can say a lot more than words
by the direction of you feet.
Are you quick to run to scandal, sin and pride?
Or do you run to Jesus,
the One His own denied?
Do you run to help the lost?
When they're drowning in their grief?
Do you run to help the widow,
or are you quick to forgive a thief?
Show the world you're different,
show them that you care.
Show them a heart that's filled with love
'cause Jesus'light shines there.
May each breath you take,
like the prophets of old,
Point to a coming hope and home
that they indeed foretold.
Let the pages of your life
sing out the Gospel tune
That Jesus died and rose again
and will come to take us soon!

Broken Pottery

Broken pottery lets more light through. That might sound like a trite little message in a fortune cookie, but on a serious note it's the testimony of every Christian that has suffered great pain, but given it to God.

I encourage you to look into the life of one such stalwart of the faith, Corrie ten Boom, (co-author of The Hiding Place). This pint-sized Dutch lady, and her family were central to the survival of many jews during the terrors of the holocaust and paid for it dearly- her elderly father and her frail sister, with their lives due to imprisonment and cruel treatment by the Nazis. In this amazing story, you will see that Corrie and her sister, never lost faith in God, despite the incredible ordeals they endured.

For a lot of people this would be the end of the story – that is what Satan would wish; to chalk it up on the blackboard as another one he has destroyed and defeated, but like so many testimonies to the goodness of God in the midst of trials, Corrie could say, 'but God'. God had a plan to use her pain to be a source of great healing and light in a post-war darkness. She went on to be a renowned public speaker all over the world, preaching forgiveness and healing in spite of all the atrocities she had experienced and witnessed, because she chose to forgive and invite Jesus in to every hurt, and pain. Though at times this was incredibly difficult, God was able to shine through her life and use her as an instrument

Broken Pottery (Continued)

of His great redemptive and restorative work. She later received recognition from the Yad Vashem Remembrance Authority as one of the "Righteous Among the Nations" on December 12, 1967. (United States Holocaust Memorial Mueseum n.d. :para.1).

Are you holding on to unforgiveness and can't see past it? You may think you are punishing that other person, but in fact they are continuing to hold control over your life and how you feel and a root of bitterness will start to grow in your heart. I have sadly witnessed a life taken over by this canker as it invades every area of their life and steals their joy, leaving a gnarled tree where once a beautiful garden grew. We need to forgive and guard our hearts from resentment so God's light can shine through our broken parts and we can be made whole.

Lord Jesus, I want you to shine through my life. I want to let go of all this pain and unforgiveness, but I don't know how. It's too overwhelming. Please show me how to let go and forgive those who have hurt me. You know everything I have been through and not one of my tears has escaped your notice – in fact you catch each one of my tears. Psalm 56:8. Please come into this situation and help me to be obedient and forgive ____. Please replace my anger and bitterness with compassion and love. Thank you that I have forgiven ____ even though I don't feel any different, I know I have been

Broken Pottery (Continued)

obedient and as I remind myself that I have left it in your hands, you will help me guard my thoughts against going back to a place of unforgiveness and eventually my feelings will also fall into alignment with my obedience to You.

>Proverbs 4:23
>Keep thy heart with all diligence; for out of it are the issues of life.

Tip: when old feelings of unforgiveness rise up in your chest say out loud (ideally), "Thank you Lord that I have forgiven ____. Please help me with how I am feeling and help me to see ____ as you see them and to just feel your peace." I've also found it's very hard to feel bitter or angry towards someone if I keep praying for them and ask God to work in their lives! Even now if thoughts rise at some perceived injustice I feel, however inconsequential, 'oh, so and so didn't respond in a very compassionate way' rather than let that turn into a grudge I turn it into a prayer! God bless them, bless our friendship and help me remember You are all I need!

Broken Pottery   (Continued)

Note: Never confuse forgiveness with having boundaries. According to Drs Cloud and Townsend,

> Boundaries define us. They define what is me and what is not me. A boundary shows me where I end and someone else begins, leading me to a sense of ownership. Knowing what I am to own and take responsibility for gives me freedom. If I know where my yard begins and ends, I am free to do with it what I like. Taking responsibility for my life opens up many different options. However, if I do not "own" my life, my choices and options become very limited.(CloudTownsend Resources 2016:What Do You Mean Boundaries? Me and Not Me.)

Let the Light Shine Through

I had a bag of bottles each one a different hue.
I'd been carrying them for so long,
I didn't know what to do.
Each one was old and heavy
filled with memories from the past,
of times of disappointment or of so called love
that didn't last.
Some were filled with hopes now dashed
that just weren't meant to be,
but I knew if I gave them to Jesus
a lot better it would be.
So awkwardly I handed
the whole bag over to Him,
wondering what He'd do with
my strange bag of suffering.
And then to my amazement
one sweep of His dear hand,
He'd made a beautiful light stand
that shone across the land.
For as I dared to look up
to see what He had done,
I saw each bottle shining in
the light of Him, God's Son.
The bottles once murky, dusty and alone
now moulded all together did
shine like bright gem stones!
For when you give your hurting,
your loss and pain to Him,
He'll shine His love right through it

Let the Light Shine Through   (Continued)

and heal you from within.
Then all the world will see it,
the beauty He has made
from taking those old bottles
and bringing healing for which you prayed.

Who I am

Isaiah 53:6
All we like sheep have gone astray; we have turned every one to his own way; and the LORD hath laid on him the iniquity of us all.

Who I am

I finally know who I am
When I look at Your nail-torn hands
I see the scars that made me clean
For I am loved beyond the seen
This world may see me as a loss
With no wealthy title – a life of dross
But I am so desperately loved
By Him who reigns and lives above
To Him I'm worth each precious drop
Of royal blood His body did drop
He calls me His out from my sin
He makes me new and lives within.
For my value comes not from what I've done
But who I am in Christ the Son.

His Beautiful Creation or Discarded Things?

It was my birthday and the thing that I was really looking forward to was going op-shopping! Now most people have one of two responses to buying clothes in an op-shop, 'oh no, I don't like clothes that someone else has been wearing. I only buy new' or 'I love op-shopping! You never know what you might find for a few dollars!' I definitely identify with the second group.

While thinking about this today, I wondered what it was that I loved so much about going into a store full of pre-loved goods, often in hickledy-pickeldy fashion, and searching for a treasure? I said to my husband, I think it's the character of God, planted deep within us to want to restore something that has been discarded. For in an opshop there are many clothes and items that were once purchased new, and possibly at great cost now cast aside as of no use and no longer desirable. Pondering more on this thought, it really hit me, how as broken people we can feel like these discarded things.

We may have been really loved by our parents when we were young, but the older us, with individual opinions and values doesn't suit their controlling nature. It may be that a partner left us for someone they like better. It may be that our whole life we have felt 'overlooked' as someone else always gets the promotion, the praise or the presents and we wonder, 'what's wrong with me? Aren't I good enough?'

His Beautiful Creation or Discarded Things? (Continued)

But this is the really cool truth I want to share today and if we can grab hold of this, well it changes everything! Just like me in the opshop gasping with excitement over that designer brand skirt that will look great with x,y and z, God gasps with excitement over you! Not because you look great hanging there on that old wire coathanger for $2 but because He sees you as His special creation and not what you may be now but what He created you to be!

On the flipside of this, the Bible says that Jesus "was numbered with the transgressors" (Isaiah 53:12b) referring to the time He was on the cross. Think of it – the Holy Son of God, the Creator of all things, treated like a common criminal and nailed to a cross. Very few people who met Him understood who He really was — religious leaders wanted to kill him! However, those who did have an inkling of His true value, knew when they looked at Him they were staring into the face of God. Mary Magadelene, 'a girl with a past' had some understanding of the precious gift of Jesus before her when she took a bottle of spikenard, worth a years wages to wash His feet and wipe them with her hair. Jesus said of her, "Verily I say unto you, Wheresoever this gospel shall be preached in the whole world, there shall also this, that this woman hath done, be told for a memorial of her" (Matthew 26:13).

His Beautiful Creation or Discarded Things?

Ephesians 2:10
For we are his workmanship, created in Christ Jesus unto good works, which God before ordained that we should walk in them.

His Beautiful Creation or Discarded Things? (Continued)

Dear Lord, thank you that I am not unwanted, discarded or insignificant. I am in fact, Your masterpiece and You have good things planned for me to do – even before the creation of the world! Holy Spirit speak the truth over me as I nail these lies to the cross and leave them there. I know there's been people in my life that have helped to cement these lies about my value that are contrary to Your Word and ask now, in Jesus Mighty Name, to break up this foundation of lies and plant Your truth in my heart and help me to share it with others!

A great in-vest-ment?
Back in 2014, an American couple, Sean & Rikki McEvoy, purchased an old sweater from an opportunity shop for 58c. They had a business buying and selling old retro clothing online. The sweater appeared to be a bit worn, so husband Sean kept it for himself. Imagine his suprise when watching a documentary on a legendary football coach of the Green Bay Packers during the 60s and he noticed him wearing an identical jumper. Long story short, it turns out it was one and the same and at auction sold for over $43k USD! Isn't it amazing how quickly perspective can change when the true value of something is known? Who do you think knows your true value – the world or the One who made you? (Poughkeepsie Journal 2015: Westpoint Sweater Worn by Lombardi purchased at Goodwill).

The Apple of His Eye

Psalm 17:5-8
Hold up my goings in thy paths, that my footsteps slip not. I have called upon thee, for thou wilt hear me, O God: incline thine ear unto me, and hear my speech. Shew thy marvellous lovingkindness, O thou that savest by thy right hand them which put their trust in thee from those that rise up against them. Keep me as the apple of the eye, hide me under the shadow of thy wings.

Zechariah 2:8
For thus saith the Lord of hosts; After the glory hath he sent me unto the nations which spoiled you: for he that toucheth you toucheth the apple of his eye.

'îyshôwn = 'little man, pupil' אִישׁוֹן HEBREW (Strong's #380) Bible Hub; Strong's Concordance (n.d.) 380.ishon,

ba·vat ey·no = 'the apple of my eye' HEBREW Jerusalem Prayer Team (n.d.) "Hebrew Word of the Day,

The Apple of His Eye

There is One that loves you
and He calls you by name,
to leave your doubts and disappointments
and find relief from sin and pain.
For He knows you're hurting,
He sees each tear you cry.
When you stop and hear His voice that's saying,
"You're the apple of my eye!"

If we look in the verses to the left, you'll see two instances that use the phrase 'apple of the eye' and the Hebrew word and definition below it. The term 'little man' refers to the image we see of ourself reflected in the eye of another. So to think of ourselves reflected in God's eye, this means that His eye has to be on us to give the reflection. I find this very comforting to know His eye is on me. And if we think about how naturally and quickly we will move to protect our eyes, through shutting our eyes or moving our hands or arms to block our face when danger strikes, or how careful we are to protect our eyes when their is dust or debris blowing about, and how precious our eyes are to us, you can begin to grasp just how precious we are to God!

Abundant Life You Can Find

It's not on the high street,
where the main traffic flows.
It's not in the cafe's of the rich
and nosey-knows,
but down an alley way,
through a pass that's quite tight,
a quiet street – the Way of Right.
Not a lot head down that way,
they'd rather cheat and gambles play,
But I was drawn by my heart,
for something felt needed right from the start.
So down the lonely, quiet road,
I made my way to His abode.
It wasn't fancy or brightly signed
though clearly labelled and well designed.
The gate was made of timber, gold
as I drew closer, it was quite a sight to behold.
For though it didn't shout, "look at me"
you could tell it was exquisite carpentry.
Inside the gate I felt such peace,
I heard the birds – the ducks and geese
Honkering around a stooped old man,
his garments modest and wrinkled hands,
but when He turned and looked at me,
I felt I saw eternity.
For eyes so piercing swept through my soul,
but they didn't judge or harshly scold.
In fact the love that flowed from them,
moved down my spine and up again.
For none had ever gazed on me so,
but rather made me feel cheap and low

Abundant Life You Can Find   (Continued)

Who was this one so unassuming
to love me so without presuming.
This gave me courage to blurt right out
and ask with quivering stutter and shout
"Are you the One I've been looking f-for?
The One who the br-broken restores?
All my life I've known I was yearning
for something more and despite all my earning
Nothing has made me feel complete,
nothing has tasted lasting and sweet.
I've been down all the streets in this town,
Pride Lane, Riches Court and Clown Around,
but none of them produced any lasting effect.
I always went home to sadness, neglect,
but then today, I saw your sign
that said 'abundant life you can find!'
It sounded so simple and inviting,
I followed it here despite misgiving fighting.
For how could anyone offer that?
Especially in a street that's neither this or that!
Your house is nice but not really fancy
and look at your hands
their wrinkled and pierced.
What happened to you to have wounds so fierce?"
He placed his strong hand on my shoulder,
very strong for one so much older
And said, "Come sit and let me tell,
how you can have life and avoid hell as well.
For these wounds you see in my hands,
were always part of my Father's plan.
For a long-time ago, your people did sin

Abundant Life You can Find   (Continued)

and turned from my love without, within.
They broke God's holy law
and so couldn't be,
in His presence for eternity.
In times past an animal would pay
for their sin and so cleanse them that day,
but this was only a representation
of someone who'd come to their own sinful nation
He would be perfect, a lamb without spot;
that lamb was me – the Holy Son of God.
I came down from Heaven, willingly to die
so people like you could see God eye to eye.
No longer separated by the great distance
between Holy God and man's evil existence.
Now if you trust me, that burden you carry
can be wiped away and please don't tarry!
I have already paid the price for your sin
and now if you trust Me
I'll make you brand new within."
I started to cry like never before
here was the One who opened to Heaven the door
For through Him I could be made whole,
set free from my sin and have purified my soul!
I threw myself onto His chest
and felt His beard tickle as I cried my request,
"Yes, I believe!
You are the One who alone can give me new life,
free me from self, sin and strife.
Come into my heart and take over my life,
so I can have peace and be free from this town!"

Abundant Life You can Find   (Continued)

And with that, all my emptiness fled
for my heart had been filled
by love perfect and good.
For here He was, God in the flesh,
but now He looked young – in fact the best!
For now I realised the lies in my head,
saw him as old, outdated and dead.
And now I knew God was alive,
and Jesus had come —a real Man by my side!
Now with His help, I'd walk day by day
and stay at His house, eat together and pray.
For though the rest of the town
would try and lure me,
it's Jesus I wanted for He had pursued me.
For now looking back, with joy I could see
all the time I was **seeking**, He was seeking me.

Who's Your Influencer? Part 1

Daniel 3:4-6
Then an herald cried aloud, To you it is commanded, O people, nations, and languages, That at what time ye hear the sound of the cornet, flute, harp, sackbut, psaltery, dulcimer, and all kinds of musick, ye fall down and worship the golden image that Nebuchadnezzar the king hath set up: And whoso falleth not down and worshippeth shall the same hour be cast into the midst of a burning fiery furnace.

Daniel 3:16-17
Shadrach, Meshach, and Abednego, answered and said to the king, O Nebuchadnezzar, we are not careful to answer thee in this matter. If it be so, our God whom we serve is able to deliver us from the burning fiery furnace, and he will deliver us out of thine hand, O king. But if not, be it known unto thee, O king, that we will not serve thy gods, nor worship the golden image which thou hast set up.

Who's Your Influencer? Part 1

I think back to the amazing story of three courageous, young Jewish men who would not bow to a pagan god despite the whole world prostrating themselves before this man-made image and the ruling king demanding absolute obedience and hommage to him and his golden statue. This was the story of Shadrach, Meschach and Obednego in Daniel Chapter 3 of the Old Testament, in the year, 597bc. These young men, taken as captives from the land of Israel and now living in foreign Babylon, are expected to bow to the customs and religion of this pagan land, including worshipping their idols and false gods. Imagine the pressure these young guys felt!

Today, it's not so obvious when we are pressured into following the world or other people's ideas and plans for our lives. It can be obvious, but often it's subtle, controlling and manipulative behaviour that influences how we see ourselves, God and others. It could be a social media influencer that appears to have all the answers and we feel a heavy burden to mimic them and strive to be like them. They are the beautiful, the strong, the successful. There also may be people in our lives who want us to bow to their rule, to submit to their authority and their idea of how things should be done and will make it very uncomfortable when we don't comply or try to think for ourselves.

Who's Your Influencer? Part 1 (Continued)

We may have grown up with very controlling family or have controlling people still in our lives that don't recognise boundaries or refuse to, and have a way of treading us down, keeping us under their thumb and under their thinking. Like this king, King Nebuchadnezzar, their rules and behaviour benefit them and fit within their mentality of how things should be – how you should be. These strong, controlling behaviours can be very hard to identify and break free from but with God's help we can identify these toxic relationships and learn how to set healthy boundaries for ourselves.

Dear Lord, thank you for the courage of Shadrach, Meschach and Abednego to honour You and follow Your ways no matter the cost. Please give us courage like this and show us any relationships where we need to be set free and stand up for You. In Jesus' name, Amen.

Who's your Influencer? Part 2

Shadrach, Meschach and Abednego loved God and sought His approval rather than man's and refused to go against the commandment of the Lord that said, "Thou shalt not make unto thee any graven image, or any likeness of any thing that is in heaven above, or that is in the earth beneath, or that is in the water under the earth: thou shalt not bow down thyself to them, nor serve them" (Exodus 20:4a). They let God be their Influencer, rather than man and whether we realise it or not, we all have 'influencers' in our lives —whether they be good or bad.

Do you have people in your life that are continuing to have a negative impact on your mental health and wellbeing? Or are your influencers pulling you in a unhealthy direction. Do they treat you differently when you choose to make your own decisions that don't necessarily align with theirs? Or people you follow on social media who make you feel anxious and inadequate when you see their latest post on Instagram that makes them look so fantastic without a care in the world.

Who's Your Influencer? Part 2 (Continued)

My advice is to prayerfully consider the influencers in your life: family, friends, co-workers, social media 'mega-influencers' and consider whether these people are drawing you closer to Jesus or away from Him. Do they encourage you to seek the Lord's direction on decisions you make or do they tell you what you should do - even if you haven't asked? Do they fill your cup or do they deplete it and leave you feeling inadequate?

One thing I noticed with my toxic influencer was the need to work hard to please them, to show them I am worthy of love and approval, but always feeling I never quite measured up. That's definitely a sign of an unhealthy relationship or at least an unhealthy drive on my part to want to earn another person's approval and affection.

Firstly, our hearts should belong to Jesus (Ephesians 3:17-19) and be concerned with what He thinks of us and how we can please Him. We can find out how to do this through prayer, reading His Word, listening to His Spirit and asking godly believers for advice (making sure it lines up with the Bible), and secondly if we have to continually work to earn someone's love then this quite possibly isn't someone we should be letting influence us. If we're not feeling loved and accepted by them as we are, they may be using our striving for their own gain.

Who's Your Influencer? Part 2 (Continued)

If you're not sure that the influence someone has in your life is healthy or coming from a good place, I would prayerfully consider seeking out a Christian counsellor or pastor who should be able to give you impartial advice and ask the Lord to guide you.

Ephesians 3:17-19
That Christ may dwell in your hearts by faith; that ye, being rooted and grounded in love,
May be able to comprehend with all saints what is the breadth, and length, and depth, and height; And to know the love of Christ, which passeth knowledge, that ye might be filled with all the fulness of God.

Who's Your Influencer? Part 3

Matthew 11:28-29
Come unto Me all ye that labour and are heavy laden and I will give you rest. Take my yoke upon you and learn of Me for I am meek and lowly in heart: and ye shall find rest unto your souls.

Jesus calls those that 'labour' and are 'heavy laden' or weighed down to take on His yoke, for it is easy. The yoke is the big crosspiece put on the neck of two cows and attached to a large tool in order to plow a field for example. Why would Jesus say His yoke is easy? Well when you consider that when we become His child He promises to never leave us or forsake us (Hebrews 13:5), He assures in 1 Peter 5:7 that we can "cast all our care upon Him, for He careth for you." and in Psalm 28:7 says, He is our strength and shield; then in this context, are we really carrying the yoke or is it more like a father 'letting' his child help carry the heavy bag of shopping? The child is holding on to the bag, thinking they are so strong, but the father, in fact is bearing all the weight. For if we consider that He is always with us, we can cast all our worries onto Him and He is our strength and shield, then of course He can say 'my yoke is ... light.' He has already won our victory at the cross, He promises to sustain us everyday and His love for us is not based on our performance or on our benefit to Him, but rather His true love —sacrificial love that gives without taking and

Who's your influencer? Part 3 (Continued)

only wants us to love Him and grow in relationship with Him. He truly is a loving Father to His children! So don't dance to the world's drum. Listen to the voice of the Lord, follow His ways and you will experience joy, peace and love that the world can't even comprehend! Let Him alone be your influencer! *See note regarding narcissistic people next page.

Dear Lord, please show me who are the influencers in my life. Show me who I am letting speak into my heart and whether they are drawing me to or from you. Please forgive me if I have let fear of people and their opinions influence my decisions and actions. Help me rather spend more time with you, in your Word, in prayer, in quiet reflection and in fellowship with other Christ-followers in order to truly follow you and let you influence EVERY part of my life; for I know it is in doing this that I will be filled to overflowing by Your love and Your presence and make decisions out of faith and love rather than fear.

*Note about dealing with narcissitic or difficult people:

Don't get me wrong, as Christians we should show love and compassion to everyone – even those who don't return it, but we need to be careful to guard our hearts (Proverbs 4:23). Firm boundaries are needed to ensure the decisions we make are what Jesus is leading us to make and not what people around us are expecting and pressuring us to make. For these three young Jewish men, who were quite possibly in their late teens, the pressure to comply and fit in with the culture and those in charge would have been immense but, as we saw earlier their hearts belonged to God and it was Him that spoke to their hearts and led their decisions.

Beyond God's Love?

Do you believe you're beyond God's love?
You too low, Him high above.
Your grasp is small, but His is great.
Trust Him now —it's not too late.
He loves you more than words can say.
Call out to Him —He hears you pray.

Ephesians 3:16-21
That he would grant you, according to the riches of his glory, to be strengthened with might by his Spirit in the inner man; That Christ may dwell in your hearts by faith; that ye, being rooted and grounded in love, May be able to comprehend with all saints what is the breadth, and length, and depth, and height; And to know the love of Christ, which passeth knowledge, that ye might be filled with all the fulness of God. Now unto him that is able to do exceeding abundantly above all that we ask or think, according to the power that worketh in us, Unto him be glory in the church by Christ Jesus throughout all ages, world without end. Amen.

The Little Pottery Vase

I found a small oddly shaped pottery vase in the corner of the cutlery draw. It pulled at my heart, for it made me ask, "Did I really have a daughter? Or was that some fanciful figment of my imagination? The question startled me and confounded my simultaneously. I thought how ridiculous – of course I had a daughter! She filled every moment of my life for 18 and half years. I can even now think back on memories of our life together, but at the same time I ask did any of it even really happen? Am I somehow caught in a great conspiracy, had my mind 'played with' to think I was once a mother, once held a role of guide and protector, provider and counsellor. Once had a little genetic copy of myself, so similar and yet so different. Did I just make up all those memories? For now looking at that little funny vase in the draw, upon which I can barely make out the words, "Dear Mum, Happy Mother's Day, Exxx) I feel so strangely disconnected. For this and random photos that burst through my social media scrolling, declare that there was a life embedded in mine and slowly torn away. It sounds absurd to question such reality or even to admit my brain would question me on such a significant part of my existence, but as I look around me and have no knowledge of my Exxx or how she fares, I can only hope that my figment will feel the same loss as I and seek me out.

The Little Pottery Vase

As always, with these rambling thoughts I have, I'm led back to my dear Father in Heaven and how it feels for Him to be abandoned by His creation, His children. There is a whole world out there, milling around in aimless existence, chasing and loving the created rather than the Creator. He at least knows where each one of them is and what they are up to, but none the less must experience great sorrow to be disconnected from those He intricately made and loves.

What about you? Are you connected to your Creator? He yearns to hold you close, to forgive you of all you sins and to make you whole. He yearns to commune with you as a loving Father to His child. Will you let Him? We may not have the relationship we yearn for with family or friends, but we can with God. He sent Jesus to die for our sins so we could be made perfect in love and become His child!

Ecclesiastes 12:12
Remember thy Creator in the days of thy youth, while the evil days come not, nor the years draw nigh, when thou shalt say, I have no pleasure in them.

References

Bible Hub: Strong's Concordance (n.d.) 380.ishon
https://biblehub.com/hebrew/380.htm

CloudTownsend Resources (9 March 2016) What Do You Mean Boundaries? CloudTownsend Resources, accessed 21 June 2024.
https://www.cloudtownsend.com/what-do-you-mean-boundaries-by-dr-henry-cloud-and-dr-john-townsend/

Jerusalem Prayer Team (n.d.) Hebrew Word of the Day, Jerusalem Prayer Team, accessed 11 July 2024.
https://hebrew.jerusalemprayerteam.org/apple-ones-eye/

Warner Bros Entertainment (2014) The Lego Movie, Burbank, CA.

Poughkeepsie Journal (10 February 2015) Westpoint Sweater Worn by Lombardi Purchased at Goodwill, Gannett News Service, accessed 10 June 2024.
https://www.poughkeepsiejournal.com/story/sports/2015/02/10/west-point-sweater-worn-lombardi-purchased-goodwill/23185489/

Scripture References taken from the King James Version of the Bible.
https://www.kingjamesbibleonline.org/
Original work published 1769)

United States Holocaust Memorial Mueseum (n.d.) "Corrie ten Boom." Holocaust Encyclopedia.
https://encyclopedia.ushmm.org/content/en/article/corrie-ten-boom. Accessed on 24 June 2024

About the Author

Bronwyn lives with her husband, Patrik full time in their caravan, travelling around Australia, wherever God leads them. She is a registered nurse, but loves writing, drawing and designing Christian greeting cards and products, and is excited for where God will take this in the future. Her heart is that everyone will know how much Jesus truly loves them and find their purpose in Him!

Check out her other exciting book, about a leper whose life is changed forever when he meets 'That Super Awesome Guy!' Available online from all major bookstores and Amazon.

THAT SUPER AWESOME GUY!

"is a relatable and captivating story. With suspense it ushers the reader into a journey from sadness to joy! The book makes anyone long to know Jesus, the healing, selfless, helpful nice man who with just one touch can change your life. Surely it's a story for everyone!"

PATRICIA – PARENT, UGANDA NOW IN AUSTRALIA

www.ingramcontent.com/pod-product-compliance
Lightning Source LLC
Chambersburg PA
CBHW041148110526
44590CB00027B/4168